Kai Talks About the Missions

by Angel Heart

POOR Press

ISBN 978-1-7329250-9-0

Thank you to POOR Press team for design and copy-editing

**A POOR Press Publication © 2021.
All Rights Reserved.**

POOR Press is a poor and indigenous people-led press dedicated to publishing the books and scholarship of youth, adults, and elders in poverty locally and globally.

**www.poormagazine.org
www.poorpress.net**

This book is dedicated to all First Nations Peoples, their ancestors, or Eguns, and to my beloved Ochosi.

Maferefun Ochosi! Ashe'!

Introduction

Truth telling in history is almost never what we learn in school when it comes to First Nations Peoples. If you go online to do a search of the mission system, you're most likely to find language with such words as, "dynamic, humble, honor, quest, untamed-wilderness, thriving, royal, and empire," to describe the history of California Missions (CA.gov).

In this second installment of a series by Angel Heart, Author & Activist, Kai explains the truth about California Missions, and what his ancestors, the Lisjan Ohlone Peoples, endured. Inspired by the need for children to learn the truth about this land, and with permission from Corrina Gould, the Traditional Spokesperson for the Confederated Villages of Lisjan, this book was created as a sequel to *HorŠe Tuuxi, My name is Kai.*

HorŠe Tuuxi, it's Kai from Huichin! In the last book, *HorŠe Tuuxi, My name is Kai*, I taught you that HorŠe Tuuxi means 'good day.' You may also remember that Huichin or Oakland, California, is one of the territories me and my ancestors are from. The Ohlone have lived in Huichin and the East Bay since the beginning of time. We are First Nations Peoples and protectors of the earth.

In the villages of my ancestors, everything was made from nature, so everything was biodegradable. It went back into the earth to nourish the land. My Ohlone ancestors never took too much from Mother Earth and understood, if they took care of the land, the land would take care of them. My ancestors lived peacefully for thousands of years until Spanish Colonizers arrived.

Spanish Colonizers used violence to commit genocide. Violence is when someone uses force to scare, hurt and kill. Genocide is the deliberate killing of many people in a particular culture, tribe or nation. Lisjan Ohlone land was stolen through genocide and violence.

In 1546, Juan Rodríguez Cabrillo, a Spanish Maritime Explorer, was on a ship coming down the coast of what is now called California; and claimed the land for the Spanish crown. He called "dibs," having never left the ship to step on land. (Cabrillo never even met the Ohlone peoples). He died a few days later and the Spanish left.

When Spain came back in the 1700s, they were afraid they were going to lose the land Cabrillo had claimed for the Spanish Crown. Spain knew that violence worked because they had already committed genocide in Mexico. Spain wanted Ohlone land too, so the Spanish Crown appointed Junipero Serra, a priest in the catholic church. Serra went from what is now San Diego, to the Bay Area, to steal the Ohlone land the Spanish called "dibs" on.

As these colonizers went up and down the coast, they used violence to enslave my ancestors as a workforce. My ancestors built Mission Dolores in what is now San Francisco and Mission San Jose in what we now call Fremont, California. My ancestors were forcibly baptized in the catholic church and were prevented from returning home to their villages.

My ancestors worked day and night to build the missions and were forced to sleep in cold, dark spaces with nothing to call their own. The Ohlone Peoples were forbidden from speaking their languages and were forced to do catholic prayers. My Ohlone ancestors wanted to speak our languages, sing our songs, dance our dances, and teach Ohlone children about our culture; like my people always have. Some Ohlone ancestors chose to fight back.

In another act of violence, the Spanish colonizers brought animals that were not Indigenous to this land. These animals were grazers placed onto Ohlone lands. Cows, sheep, goats, donkeys, and pigs polluted the land, which changed the waterways. The grazing animals ate the plants that were my ancestors' food and medicines. My ancestors needed these plants and clean water ways to survive and stay healthy.

My ancestors were also introduced to foods that made them sick; and since the medicines were grazed away, my ancestors couldn't get better. My ancestors were made sick from diseases the Spanish brought, like smallpox and typhoid. The catholic church brought disease, starvation, and murder to the Ohlone people.

When Ohlone land was stolen to create California, some of the first laws made it illegal to be First Nations (Native American or Indian). California spent 1.4 million dollars killing First Nations Peoples. Colonizing settlers were given $5 for the head, and 25 cents for the ears of Ohlone Indians they'd killed.

Today, kids in 4th grade history class learn about First Nations; of the land that we now call California. Kids learn how my people "used to" dress, what we "used to" eat and how we "used to" live – not realizing that the Ohlone are still here. Then, when kids go to the 5th grade, they learn about the California Gold Rush and never hear, or continue to learn, about my ancestors anymore.

Children aren't learning how my ancestors were hunted down or how California laws continued to harm my ancestors. They're not learning about bounties. Did you know that a bounty is a sum of money paid for killing or capturing a person or people? My Ohlone Ancestors were killed for bounties. Ohlone children were kidnapped and sold into slavery ($300 for girls, $180 - $200 for boys).

My ancestors had to go into hiding and had to pretend they weren't Ohlone, so they could save their own lives. My Ohlone ancestors stayed hidden for a very long time because they were afraid. The Ohlone Elders were scared to talk about who they were as a people. My ancestors were afraid of going to jail for being Ohlone; frightened of the terrible things that were continuing to happen to them. Colonization disrupted my peoples' peaceful way of living.

In less than 100 years, the genocide of Ohlone peoples led to 90% of my people losing our lives and our lands..….But my people are strong! The Ohlone are still here! We are reawakening our languages and teaching the next generation of Ohlone children. This is why my Grandma speaks out and works hard every day to teach others about Ohlone land and our people.

My Grandma is working to save our Shellmounds and to get back our stolen land. She believes in truth-telling-in-history and says, "Our people have always been here." My Grandma honors our ancestors and so do I! I'm Kai, and I'm proud to be a strong Lisjan Ohlone!

Glossary

Ancestors - family/relatives that lived before us, who have passed away.

Baptized - an action taken to admit someone into a particular church.

Biodegradable - an item, substance or object that can be broken down into increasingly smaller pieces by bacteria, fungi or microbes; to be reabsorbed by the surrounding environment, without causing any pollution.

Colonizer - a person or people from Europe who violently stole First Nations People and their land.

Disease - a disorder of structure/function in a human, animal, or plant not caused by physical injury, which adversely affects a person or group of people.

First Nations - any of the groups of Indigenous peoples or original inhabitants of Canada, North America, Central America, and South America.

Generation - all of the people born and living at the same time.

Honor - high esteem; great respect.

HorŠe Tuuxi - (hor-sh-e-too-he) Chochenyo Ohlone word: "Good Day."

Huichin - (Hoo-ch-en) Ohlone village site now referred to as: Oakland, Alameda, Berkeley, Emeryville, Albany and Piedmont, California.

Illegal - forbidden by law.

Indigenous - originating or occurring naturally in a particular place; native.

Indigenous peoples, also referred to as first people, aboriginal people, native people, or autochthonous people, are culturally distinct ethnic groups who are native to a place which has been colonized/settled by another ethnic group.

Shellmound - sacred burial sites of First Nations/Ohlone Peoples.

Spanish Crown - Spain's government or monarchy; king and/or queen.

Spanish Missions - a series of buildings in different locations across what is now called California, which were made by Ohlone Peoples, with the intention of them being used by the catholic church.

Starvation - suffering or death caused by hunger.

Photo Credits

Front Cover & Page 16: Ohlone Village - Pre-European Contact by www.parks.smcgov.org (Mural by Artist - Ann Thiermann)

Page 7: Kai holding *HorŠe Tuuxi, My Name is Kai*, photo by Deja Gould

Page 8: Ohlone Ancestors by www.oaklandplanninghistory.weebly.com

Page 9: Spanish Mission Soldiers by www.allposters.com

Page 10: Ohlone Village/s by the bay by www.ipocshellmoundwalk.homestead.com

Page 11: No Sainthood for Serra/ Mission Dolores by www.missionlocal.org (Native American protesters decry canonization of Junipero Serra by Joe Rivano Barros)

Page 12: Enslaved Ohlone at the Missions by www.change.org

Page 13: Mission Resistance by www.facebook.com (Open Source - Free Public Content)

Page 14: Enslaved Ohlone with plow at the Missions by www.wikipedia.com

Page 15: Enslaved Ohlone at the Missions by www.wikipedia.com

Page 16: Ohlone Village; Pre-European Contact by www.parks.smcgov.org (Mural by Artist - Ann Thiermann)

Page 17: Ohlone Big Time Event by www.flikr.com

Page 18: Ohlone Boy/Children @ a Big Time Event by www.ronniesawesomelist.com

Page 19: Ruth Orta - Family Photo Display @ C.E. Smith Museum of Anthropology on the Cal State East Bay Campus in Hayward, CA. www.eastbaytimes.com (photo by Paul Kuroda)

Page 20: Corrina Gould & Ruth Orta www.facebook.com (Open Source - Free Public Content - Ohlone history discussion/speakers panel photo by Norm Sands)

Page 21: (Left to Right) Kai, Deja, Chata, Amni and Corrina Gould by www.facebook.com (Open Source- Free Public Content)

Angel Heart, Quechua-Puna, is the former Secretary and Public Relations Officer for Sacred Sites Protection and Rights of Indigenous Tribes. She was with the Vallejo, CA-based organization from 2013 – 2020. Angel Heart led and assisted in the removal of 6 Native American mascots in Solano, Contra Costa, and Napa County public schools. She currently works with POOR Magazine/Homefulness in Huichin/Oakland, CA. Angel Heart was honored at the 2019 Vallejo Pow-Wow for her contributions to First Nations Communities. She is a United States Army Veteran, with an honorable discharge, and Grandmother of 4.

Acknowledgements

I would first like to acknowledge and thank Kai, Deja, and Corrina Gould for the blessing of being permitted to write this book. I appreciate the time, attention, and all of the reviews they have made to my work. Their family is an inspiration to many. I was surely blessed the day I met them at Sogorea Te'. It's been an honor learning about them, their people, the significance of their sacred sites, and continuing with them on this path of love and solidarity. Fifty percent of the proceeds/profits from this book benefit the Sogorea Te' Land Trust at www.sogoreate-landtrust.org

I would also like to thank POOR Press, Lisa "Tiny" Gray-Garcia, Maya Ram and A.S. Ikeda for their leadership, instruction, facilitation and copy editing of this book. I'm grateful for the entire POOR Magazine Family. A BIG Thank you to POOR Magazine Solidarity Family, and the Bank of ComeUnity Reparations for using their privilege to redistribute hoarded wealth and stolen resources. Their dedication to truth and the empowerment of poverty scholars, like me, has made this book possible.

www.ingramcontent.com/pod-product-compliance
Lightning Source LLC
Chambersburg PA
CBHW041527090426
42736CB00035B/42